AuthorHouse™
1663 Liberty Drive
Bloomington, IN 47403
www.authorhouse.com
Phone: 1 (800) 839-8640

KJV
Scripture quotations marked KJV are from the Holy Bible, King James Version (Authorized Version).
First published in 1611. Quoted from the KJV Classic Reference Bible, Copyright © 1983 by The Zondervan Corporation.

Published by AuthorHouse  10/21/2016

ISBN: 978-1-5246-4528-1 (sc)
978-1-5246-4529-8 (e)

Print information available on the last page.

Any people depicted in stock imagery provided by Thinkstock are models,
and such images are being used for illustrative purposes only.
Certain stock imagery © Thinkstock.

This book is printed on acid-free paper.

Because of the dynamic nature of the Internet, any web addresses or links contained in this book may have changed
since publication and may no longer be valid. The views expressed in this work are solely those of the author and do
not necessarily reflect the views of the publisher, and the publisher hereby disclaims any responsibility for them.

authorHOUSE®

# What if We Didn't Have to EAT?

**Miyoko Ishibashi**

## What If We Didn't Need To Eat?

What if we didn't need food and we didn't need to eat?

Our lives would be completely different.

Here's what our world might look like. Our houses would be different; we wouldn't need toilets in our restrooms. There would only be bathtubs, with lots of extra bubbles to fill the empty space where our toilet once was. There'd be no need for plumbing or plumbers. No more living with clogged up kitchen sinks and overflowing toilets from wiping lots of dirty bottoms!

Those problems would be nonexistent.

Babies wouldn't need diapers, nor would they need to be potty trained. It would save parents a lot of money and frustration.

One more good thing, no more grumbling tummies or tummy aches. In fact, we wouldn't even need a tummy. No more going to the bathroom at all and that would be great because going to the bathroom is kind of gross, and a complete waste of time! Wouldn't you agree? There are plenty of things I'd rather be doing than standing in those long lines just to go to the restroom in public places.

Would we even need sinks? Possibly not, because we usually wash our hands before eating or our face after getting food all over it! But, let's keep the sink in the bathroom, because we like cleaning our hands and face, right?

Our Mother's wouldn't need to complain about us kids anymore. "Place your napkins on your lap, please." "Wipe your face, it's dirty." And, remember this one? "Don't forget to eat your veggies!" It would be one less complaint to my already full ears! "Oops, sorry Mom, just kidding." Maybe we kids should write a book, "What If Mom Didn't Complain Anymore?"

The Environmental Tree Lovers would be so happy, because there wouldn't be a need for cutting down more trees to make paper cups, paper plates, toilet paper and napkins. Kids like wiping faces on shirt sleeves, because it's so quick and easy! And wiping fingers all over our pants is oh so convenient! If we didn't do this, our clothes would stay clean and we can't have that for goodness sake! If they stay clean, we might have to wear them another day just to save water!

Our homes would be much smaller, (like tiny houses that my Dad is making right now. They're so popular, we call them Tumbleweed Houses). There'd be no need for kitchens or dining rooms with table and chairs; they'd be obsolete. I guess all we would have are bedrooms and extra bubble bathtub rooms, and maybe a library full of books for learning and studying the Bible and Creation. That would be awesome. Other than that, though, our homes would be boring and stark. No more prayers of grace and thanksgiving for our food each meal. I would miss those special prayers with family, and Thanksgiving Dinner, Christmas, Hanukkah, Passover and Birthday parties with yummy cake and ice cream. No more Halloween Trick or Treating or Valentine's candy for chocolate lovers. We wouldn't need bowls, plates, pots and pans, or silverware, that once was set on the dining room table or Dad's barbecue.

OH, NO! DAD'S FAMOUS BARBECUE WOULD BE GONE!

That wouldn't be fun at all, especially on hot summer evenings or on the 4th of July.

Hmm, we also wouldn't have to hear those funny, poofy sounds, and smell those yucky, smelly smells that usually come from Dad. Those poofy sounds are really loud, and they sound like ducks quacking!

The most important thing about not eating is that there wouldn't be starvation anywhere in the world! That would be wonderful! No more diabetes, no more obesity and no more over eating of candy that just gives us toothaches and cavities! Having no more dental appointments would be nice. It would eliminate extra stress off the parents and kids. No more painful root canals, or dentures, or implants. Who loves going to the dentist, anyway?

Raise your hand way up high, if you like going to the dentist?

Maybe we wouldn't even need to brush our teeth! Wouldn't that be nice?

To think, all these things would be eliminated
from our lives, just by taking food away.

Oh! And there'd be no more supermarkets that used to be fully stocked with our favorite foods. I wouldn't have to help Mom put all those heavy groceries away. I also wouldn't get the favor of helping Mom pick out at the snacks and drinks in our favorite market; like mint chocolate chip ice cream, and all the fresh fruits and vegetables that Mom use to buy. Going grocery shopping was a journey, especially when we shopped hungry; it meant buying more junk food like potato chips instead of apples.

Now, let's talk about going out to our favorite yummy restaurants, where we always loved going after Sunday Church service. We all had our favorite yummy pancakes and chicken pasta.

Wait a minute?

I forgot! There'd be no restaurants!

Hmm, let's think about this for a moment...

This would mean no restaurants worldwide!

They would be all gone; EXTINCT!

Everything would change, which means, we'd have less places to go.

There'd be no more coffee houses. No more fast food places.

Kids are not going to be happy about not getting their 'Happy meals'.

They aren't going to be pleased, with this change, especially at lunch time, when our tummies would be growling. Wait a minute, that's right! No lunch! No food! No tummies! Which also means; no more yummy popcorn!

You remember all that extra butter, it tastes so good. Remember watching movies on television on Friday night, family time, kicking our shoes off and really being relaxed with not a care in the world?

Don't forget about memories of going to the movie theatres eating popcorn, candy, hot dogs and Slurpee's.

There'd be no more crinkling sounds of people opening their boxes of candy and slurping the bottom of their soda cups.

My Dad hates going to the movies because he dislikes those horrible, agitating, sounds of smacking, crunching, and just hearing people eat, eat and eat, so I know one person who'd be happy about not eating at the theatres.

My Mom, is the number 1 popcorn lover. She is the only one I know who will go to the theatre just to buy the popcorn without seeing a movie. She wouldn't really like the idea of not having popcorn in our world. My mom is having withdrawals at the thought of going without eating popcorn, right now.

Hmm, what about our farm land?

There'd be no need for farmland, nor cows grazing, nor chickens, or chicken eggs, etc., no more backyard gardens.

How sad would that be? It would be especially sad for people who love planting new seeds and watching them grow into beautiful fruits and vegetables, then picking them at harvest time to share the bounty that God created for us to enjoy with our friends and family. There is great fulfillment in sharing and enjoying the fruits of our labor.

Remember being the "Hostess with the Mostest" and offering guests something to drink and eat from the beautiful array of fruit from the garden or Farmer's Market? That would be a thing of the past. No longer could we enjoy the favorite pass time where all the local farmers would sell their fresh organic peaches, apples, corn, zucchini, lettuce, fresh peanuts, strawberries, fresh farm eggs, apricots, tomatoes, squash, pumpkins, plums, grapes, watermelons, onions and all the variety of fruits and vegetables not mentioned here, for this list can go on and on... just thinking about the sweet, tangy pineapple makes our mouths water with such temptation.

"Mmm, if only we could just take a bite, but
we wouldn't, because we don't eat!

We wouldn't dare touch the fruit! It would be like in the Garden of Eden at the beginning of time when God told Adam not to eat from the tree of the knowledge of good and evil. When Eve wandered into the garden, she was tempted by the desire for such knowledge. See Genesis chapter 2 in the Bible. A serpent came along and encouraged her to disobey God saying, "Surely you won't die," so she took a bite and then gave some to Adam. In that moment, they both sinned against God and because of it we all know and experience good and evil.

Did you know the Bible is God's Word and it has fruit for our Spirit? Yep! That's right? In Galatians 5:22-23, it says the fruits of the Spirit are:

Love

Joy

Peace

Patience

Kindness

Goodness

Faithfulness

Gentleness

Self-Control

Do you have those divine fruits in your life? They're exceedingly wonderful fruits to have and to share.

We can enjoy the Fruits of the Spirit anytime, especially when we need them! And thankfully we can enjoy fruit for our bodies too.

## IF WE DIDN'T NEED TO EAT...

It would be boring. Life would be very boring without enjoying the pleasures of eating snacks, especially while watching a movie. Without having snacks, going to a sporting event or concert would be very different. Wouldn't you agree? THINK ABOUT IT... No more food vendors walking around selling goodies calling out, "Hot dogs! Soda! Peanuts! Popcorn! Candy apples! Cotton candy!" And no more jumping with excitement, waving your hands in the air to get their attention and purchase your favorite snack.

Back at home, our hospitable ways would be very limited. We'd just be sitting around in the living room when company came over; sitting on the couch, crossing our hands and thinking to ourselves, "Will someone please serve some me water? My mouth is kinda dry?"

Oops! Don't forget! No tummies means no water! It already feels like we're on a diet, huh? We'd feel worse than Jesus did when He fasted for 40 days and 40 nights! Did you know He fought the temptation of his fleshly desire for food by calling on our Heavenly Father? Yep that's right, and God sustained Him the whole time! He didn't need to eat anything! That is so cool!

Without food or drink, we wouldn't be asking anyone:

"Can I get you some water or something to eat?"

"Dinner is ready, go wash your hands."

"Can you stay for dinner?"

"Mommy, can I make brownies?"

"What's for dinner?"

"Who are we inviting for dinner next weekend?"

"Who's cooking Thanksgiving dinner this year?"

Kids wouldn't have to say:

"Do I have to eat that?

You wouldn't have to say those things anymore kiddos, because we don't eat anything. It makes my tummy growl like hunger pains just thinking about it.

Wow! So many things in our lives would be eliminated.

The Pros and Cons of not eating doesn't sound appealing to our hungry tummies, and doesn't really sound like fun at all, except for a few things:

Groceries are expensive, so we'd save a lot of money.

There'd be no more starvation!

God would have to find a new way to keep us all alive.

No more stinky, poofy, quack sounds that we used to laugh at for hours. I'd actually miss laughing at those, because kids love to laugh.

We wouldn't have to buy all those fragrances for our once called Bathroom because our new Extra Bubble Scrub and Tub Room would always smell fresh.

Without food, we wouldn't be able to share with a friend who says:

"Can you please share that with me?"

"Can I taste yours?"

We wouldn't be able to share our banana nut bread that Mom makes.

We wouldn't see any more cooking shows.

All these things would disappear if we didn't need to eat.

After all this talk about living without food, I think we all love it too much, and would never want to be without it!

Did you know that a long time ago, God provided food that fell from the sky? This story can be found in the Old Testament of the Bible, in Exodus chapter 16. When the children of Israel saw the food, they said to one another, "It's Manna!" And it filled them up with God's goodness, even though they forgot to be thankful for it and they acted kind of greedily. No matter what we do, God is good all the time, and all the time, God is good. Do you like being good? It feels so much better than being mad, sad, grumpy or bad.

Thankfully God made us the way we are to enjoy the fruits of the Spirits and even fruits, vegetables, fish and meats that nourish our bodies. He's so good. He also gives us the Bread of Life which is 'The Word of God!' The Bible states in John 6:35 that Jesus is the Bread of Life and He is 'The Word of God'. How can this be? What does this mean?

Well, try feasting on the Fruits of the Spirit and 'The Bread of Life' by reading the Holy Bible and learning about how God sent His son Jesus to die for us all (John 3:16, have your mommy look it up). We can all be forgiven of our sins and we can all go to heaven. Jesus is sitting at the right hand of God, Our Father. Jesus loves us so much, that whoever believes that He died for our sins, was buried and rose from the grave on the third day, shall be forgiven and have eternal life!

We all have the Bounty of The Bread and Life from God! I want to live, and eat!

I'm hungry! Yeah!

Let's go see what's in the fridge and Give Thanksgiving to God for our food.

THANK YOU GOD FOR YOUR BELOVED JESUS OF NAZARETH
WHO DWELLS IN OUR HEARTS

FOREVERMORE!

In Jesus Name, Amen.

Written by Miyoko Ishibashi

134 Mae Ave.

Pittsburg, CA.

94565

1 415 410 1142

mimimiyoko@gmail.com

John 6:32-33

My Father giveth you the true bread from Heaven. For the bread of God is which cometh down from Heaven and giveth life unto the world.

Printed in the United States
by Baker & Taylor Publisher Services